Political Plumlines

Also by Felicia Lamport

Political Plumlines

By Felicia Lamport

Cartoons by Bill Sanders

DOUBLEDAY & COMPANY, INC.
GARDEN CITY, NEW YORK
1984

Library of Congress Cataloging in Publication Data

Lamport, Felicia, 1916–
Political plumlines.

1. Political poetry, American. 2. United States—
Politics and government—1945–   —Poetry. I. Title.
PS3523.A449P6   1984   811'.54

ISBN: 0-385-18819-6
Library of Congress Catalog Card Number 82-46013

"National Anathema of 1976" is reprinted by permission of *The Bulletin of the Atomic Scientists,* a magazine of science and public affairs. Copyright © 1976 by the Educational Foundation for Nuclear Science, Chicago, Ill. 60637.
"David Frost's Interviews Produce Three New Nixons" first published in the New York *Times,* Volume 126, Number 43583, on May 22, 1977.
"Leaves of Crass" first published in the New York *Times,* Volume 130, Number 44903, on March 30, 1981.
"Sprung Lamb," "Greatest Show on Earth," and "The Love Song of R. Milhous Nixon, 1973" are reprinted by permission of Dodd, Mead & Company, Inc./Everest House from *Light Metres* by Felicia Lamport. Copyright © 1982 by Felicia Lamport.
"President Zia of Pakistan Dismisses Carter's $400,000,000 Aid Offer as Peanuts (News Item)," now entitled "Spurned Kernels," and "Exxon Sunnyside Up" first appeared in *The New Republic.*
"Look Back in Wonder at Joseph McCarthy," "Nixon Picks a New Vice-President," "Recollected in Futility," "Nixsong," "Campaign Trailings, 1983," "Brave Gnu World," "Helmsman, Spare that Ship of State!," "Subliminal Subterfuge," "En Garde," "Last Tango at Port Stanley," "June 30, 1982, Distaff Nonepitaph," "Mal de Mayor," "Rational Fashion Note, 1981," "Up a Tree," "A Reagan Primer," "The Wreck of Reagan's First Budget Plan," "Elegy to the Country's Out-of-Stockman," "Reaganalysis," "Vintage '81," "New Year's Advice to the Affluent for 1982," "Capping the Pipe," "Arms and the Salesman," "The Old Broken Budget," "Frustration," "Funeral Peroration," "Adieu, '82," "Xtravaganza," "Silver Lining," "The Rubáiyát of Omar Khayyám (in a new translation by Secretary of the Interior James G. Watt)," "'Shoot, if You Must,'" and "The Red and the Black Ink," first appeared in the Boston *Globe.*
"Marine Hmm?" and "The Shift-of-Power Hours" first appeared in the Boston *Phoenix.*

CONTENTS

The Nixon Years

The Love Song of R. Milhous Nixon, 1973   7
Nixon Picks a New Vice-President   9
Recollected in Futility   10
National Anathema of 1976   11
Nixsong   12
Marine Hmm?   14
Sprung Lamb   15
David Frost's Interviews Produce Three New Nixons   16
Look Back in Wonder at Joseph McCarthy   18

Sundry Wonders

Poll Star   19
Greatest Show on Earth   20
Helmsman, Spare that Ship of State!   21
Campaign Trailings, 1983   24
Brave Gnu World   26
Subliminal Subterfuge   27
En Garde   28
Last Tango at Port Stanley   29
June 30, 1982, Distaff Nonepitaph   30

The Jimmy Fun

Exxon Sunnyside Up   31
The Shift-of-Power Hours   32
Spurned Kernels   34

A Militance of Mayors

—and Still Mayor   35

The Byrning of Chicago: January 1982   36
Mal de Mayor   38

The Reagan Reign

Rational Fashion Note, 1981   40
Leaves of Crass   41
A Reagan Primer   44
Up a Tree   46
The Wreck of Reagan's First Budget Plan   47
Elegy to the Country's Out-of-Stockman   49
Casey at the Battlements   50
Clothes Question   51
Reaganalysis   52
Vintage '81   53
New Year's Advice to the Affluent for 1982   55
Capping the Pipe   56
Arms and the Salesman   57
The Red and the Black Ink   58
"Shoot, if You Must"   60
The Old Broken Budget   61
Dialogue   62
Frustration   64
Funeral Peroration   65
Adieu, '82   66
Xtravaganza   68
Silver Lining   69
The Rubáiyát of Omar Khayyám (in a new transla-
    tion by Secretary of the Interior James G. Watt)   70

THE LOVE SONG OF
R. MILHOUS NIXON, 1973

Let us go then, in my plane,
For a weekend of repose in Key Biscayne;
When the view beneath our eyes appears unstable
Let us banish all incipient defeats
In one of my retreats.
Come, Bebe! Join in *dolce far niente*
If not in Florida, in San Clemente.
Let us show our heels to media that prate
Endlessly of Watergate,
That plague us with their rude, insistent questions.
Oh, do not ask, "Who planned or
Covered up?" Trust in my candor.

In the polls my image ebbs, sinks low,
Buffeted by imbroglio.

But indeed there will be time
If I tough it out and never lose my cool,
Chanting my old security refrain;
There will be time to skim the slime,
Time to purge the scum-filled journalistic pool,
To send my critics swirling down the drain,
Time to nurture apathy,
And time yet for a hundred new evasions,
And time for many more "alert" occasions:
There'll be no need for me to cop a plea.

In the polls my image ebbs, sinks low,
Buffeted by imbroglio.

But I have conned them all already, conned them all,
Grown skilled in arts of masterly escape;
I have measured out my life in reels of tape.
Equipped with secrets gleaned from bugged calls,
There is no foe I cannot undermine
    So why should I resign?

No, I am not an Agnew, though my Checkered past
Includes the sour years I suffered through
My unrewarded hopes as Number Two;
Whatever small tax benefits I took
Are inadequate as recompense:
Politics require perspicuity,
Yet any man who has a grain of sense
Lays by a small and safe agnewity.
But I am not a crook.

I keep cool . . . I keep cool . . .
I shall have another thousand days to rule.

Shall I let my tapes unroll? Shall I dare them
    to impeach?
I shall triumph thanks to Rosemary's extraordinary
    reach.
I have heard my staffers peaching each on each.

I do not think that they will peach on me.

I shall weather every crisis that may loom.
What if the secrets writ in milk are spilt
And détente now seems Kissingerry-built?
I shall still command the White House Oval Room.
Disaster cannot hope to bring me down
Unless the Watergates burst open, and I drown.

NIXON PICKS A NEW VICE-PRESIDENT

What could ever have been fitter than the elegance
    and glitter
  Of the East Room all atwitter with suspense
As Dick's handpicked group of solons stood assembled
    (*nolens volens*)
  Waiting tensely for the party to commence?

He had Julie, Pat, and Tricia, plus a band from
    the militia
  To provide the proper prime-time glamour touch,
And his teasing and digressing set the audience
    to guessing:
  Would his choice be So-and-So or Such-and-Such?

Then what pleasure he afForded when he finally
    recorded
  His selection, with a twinkle so refined
Yet so fraught with magnetism that no recent Agnewism
  Could conceivably have clotted any mind.

Stonewalls did not misprision make
    Nor fired aides confess
Until the tapes began to break
    With such effectiveness
That Candor could recover from
    That bungled Operation
And rise to let the public plumb
    Oval Rumination.

NATIONAL ANATHEMA OF 1976

CIA, can you see
By the Chile dawn light
How profoundly you failed
In your secretive scheming
When your Helmsman struck shoals
And your vessel sprang leaks
As the venture was botched
Past all hope of redeeming?

Though the plot was insane
It was Kissingermane
To a high cosmic plane—
And could happen again!

CIA, may no newfangled planners enlarge
The price we have paid for today's covert charge!

NIXSONG

Dick got no kick from campaigns.
　　Given abysmal charisma like his,
How strange that he soared to success.
　　But Dick got a kick from the press.

Dick's lasting image remains:
　　Grand avatar of the secondhand car
Whose evasions could always create
　　A picture of . . . lying in state.

　　　　When any trouble came muddling in,
　　　　How fast he could outflank it,
　　　　Pulling his cover-up, cuddling in
　　　　His cosy "security" blanket!

Guarding his file and his rank,
　　Switching a Richardson into the niche
From which Mitchell was fired point-blank,
　　Dick walked on the Water—and sank.

MARINE HMM?

From the hauls of vast mazu-u-ma
    In the C.R.E.E.P.
Colson treated the consu-u-mer
    To an I.T. Tea party.

Laundered lucre in unending streams
    Made him Master of the Hunt
And a power in such merry schemes
    As the Ellsberg break-in stunt.

Though these turned out unpropitiously
    For the team he'd brought aboard,
He continued to be "viciously
    Loyal" to his overlord,

Seeking justice to obstruct till he
    Saw his cover come unstuck,
Rushing then to cop a fervent plea
    Lest he end as ground-up Chuck.

Can the man who said he'd gladly tread
    On his grandmamma for Dick
Be prepared instead to boot the head
    Of the body politic?

Will this wholesome Colson course have force
    That may prove un-breach-a-ble
As he ties in to a Higher Source
    That is un-im-peach-a-ble?

SPRUNG LAMB

After his sudden religious conversion
   One Nixon lieutenant could get off the hook
By answering any who cast an aspersion,
   "The Lord is my shepherd, and I am His crook."

DAVID FROST'S INTERVIEWS PRODUCE THREE NEW NIXONS

May 1977

The Hoosier Nixon

When the Frost is in ter Nixon
    ninety minutes by the clock,
Folks start sayin', "Fiddlesticks!" in
    ev'ry parlor on the block
As they hear the same ol' gabble
    an' the innercence pretense
That's suppose ter make the people
    rally roun' ter Dick's defense.

O it's then's the time a feller's
    gettin' fed up with the hoke
An' he starts aswitchin' channels
    ter get genuwine gun smoke
Or he gives the box a cussin'
    an' a knuckle-bruisin' sock
When the Frost is in ter Nixon
    ninety minutes by the clock.

The Miniver Cheevy Nixon

Richard M. Nixon, chilled by scorn,
    Taped up his lips as a civilian
Till he agreed to sound his horn
    For a million.

Richard kept calm and played it smart
    (Comebacks, to him, are scarcely novel),
Calling past lies "mistakes of heart,"
    Would not grovel.

Richard confessed a few small flaws,
    Brushing them off as controversial,
Vaunted his record—came a pause:
    Alpo commercial.

Richard, whose logic twists and bends,
    Challenged the facts with "I was there!"
Let down country, self, and friends—
    But not his hair.

The O Captain, My Captain Nixon

O Nixon! that Nixon! his course is not yet run.
The ship of state was listing when he ranked as Number One
But he emerged unscarred, self-purged, retaining still his
    pension
The while his myrmidons were on appeal or in detention.

    O what art! art! art!
      O how cleverly he's reached
        That prime-time slot where still he lies,
          Pardoned, unimpeached.

LOOK BACK IN WONDER
AT JOSEPH McCARTHY

Whom was it wise to eulogize
    And prudent to endorse?
Whose ratiocinations put
    McCart before McHorse?

Who made our state wisconsolate
    And tarnished army brass?
Whose puseyanimosity
    Made eggheads roll en masse?

Who used advanced roycohnaissance
    And arrant monkeyshines?
Whose merry "Point of order" chants
    Could curl the stiffest spines?

Who managed to command a spread
    With every news release?
Whose use of propaganda bred
    A million proper geese?

POLL STAR

Politicians, heart and soul,
Pay obeisance to the poll
As the holy scroll controlling every trick.
It condenses the conglomerate consensus
To the force that makes the body politick.

If the survey ratings show
That a policy ranks low,
It's *de trop* and must be promptly sacrificed.
For collectors of opinion hold dominion:
They're the spirit of our times—the pollstergeist.

The National Convention

See the scrimmage and the scrabble,
Hear the raucous rabble's babble,
   And the ribald rebels' ricocheting roar
When the Chairman pounds his gavel
Trying vainly to unravel
All the barking carking cavil
   On the floor.

Strange, the leaders seem untroubled
Though the hubbub has redoubled
   And the level of the revel is a blast,
For the mission, by tradition,
Of the party politician
Is to foster fuss and fission
   To the last.

When the Candidate is chosen
What togetherness then flow in—
   Every bourbon glass becomes a loving cup.
See the opposition crumble,
Watch the former idols tumble,
Hear that cheering laughter rumble—
   Step right up!

HELMSMAN, SPARE THAT SHIP
OF STATE!

"We must work a little faster,"
   said the Helmsman to his crew,
"To get both Houses voting
   just as Right as me and you:
Raise the anti on abortion
   and school busing everywhere,
Use ketchup as the vegetable
   on school-lunch bills of fare,
And keep the kiddies happy
   with a daily dose of prayer."

Said Orrin Hatch to Jesse Helms,
   "Though what you say is true,
Those tenets hit the Senate's floor
   and bounced in '82,
And the few we hustled through,
   the courts then set about to thwart."
Quoth Helms, "Now, Cousin, don't you fret,
   we'll cut that problem short:
We'll pass a law that will abort
   the powers of the court!"

But Orrin answered, "Jesse,
   in the '82 upset
The voters sent our candidates
   right down the *oubliette*."
"Oh, don't be borin', Orrin,
   'Twas a midterm fluke, no more.

The final grades will pour in
   in the fall of fall of '84.
We may have lost a skirmish
   but we're going to win the war."

Loud cheers from all the hearties,
   but one tar with ruddy face
Made bold to murmur, "Sir, 'tis said
   you're shaky at home base.
North Carolina thinks that your
   priorities are wacko.
They wish you'd lay off sex and work
   on cotton and tobacco."
Helms snapped, "I've soared beyond
   that puny state I represent.
The whole of this great nation
   is my real constituent,
So I'll whomp a brand-new party up
   and run for president!"

Seven canny candidates
    sitting on the fence,
All of them aspiring to
    White House residence,

Looking neither right nor left,
    hunkered in the middle,
Each prepared to speak his own
    cautious little idyll.

Comes the Springfield cattle show,
    and the plot grows thicker:
Faced with raising all that dough,
    Bumpers proves no sticker.

That leaves Alan, Ernest, Fritz,
    Reubin, Gary, John—
Which one is the bangtail to
    put your money on?

Cranston, Hollings, Askew, Glenn,
    also Mondale, Hart—
Who, without a program, can
    tell them all apart?

Programs, though, are precious few;
    candidates are vague in
Most particulars except:
    let's get rid of Reagan.

Six determined Democrats,
    docile and restrained.
Not a neck is sticking out
    though a few are craned.

Five will soon be toppled by
    grim Eumenides . . .
Who'll be left to fill those shoes
    of Teddy Kennedy's?

BRAVE GNU WORLD

The Gnu is not a handsome beast
   Nor yet, 'tis said, the brightest,
But how its power has increased
   Since it became Gnu Rightist!

Gnu Rightists live by curious rules:
   Outlandish, one must grant is
Their edict that the young in schools
   Must ape the praying mantis.

On busing and abortion, they
   Keep putting in their two cents,
And vis-à-vis the ERA
   They're just a bloody Gnuisance.

Nostalgic for the happy time
   When Agnu was in flower,
They're raising reveGnue to climb
   To true Gnuclear power.

SUBLIMINAL SUBTERFUGE

A *sub rosa* sub's been submerged in
  The bottom of Sweden's Hors Bay,
Disturbing the sturgeon converged in
  A promising Hors d'oeuvre buffet.

It's said that the sub is subversive
  Though no one can make the charge stick,
Since it's only been subtly incursive
  With a small oleaginous slick.

Though frogmen could only bring muck up,
  With bits of debris interspersed,
'Tis sworn that a snorkel was snuck up
  For air on October the first.

Since then, helicopters have hovered
  And mine traps have blocked all egress,
But the sub will no doubt be discovered
  In the fathomless depths of Loch Ness.

EN GARDE

They're changing guard at Buckingham Palace.
The home secretary may need digitalis
Since the chief palace guard has delivered a shock
Of Blunt revelations sufficient to rock
        The most callous.

They're changing guard at Buckingham Palace.
Her Majesty shows no scintilla of malice,
But Parliament's making a terrible stew . . .
There hasn't been any such hullaballoo
        Since Wallis.

LAST TANGO AT PORT STANLEY

Somewhere south of Buenos Aires and a trifle to the east
Lie two hundred rocky islets of which Britain has been
    fleeced,
But the Britons are determined to inflict the great defeat
On the captors of their kelpers with the loyal sheep that
    bleat:
  "Come you back eight thousand miles
  To reclaim your Falkland Isles!
You cannot let those gauchos give the lion's tail a tweak!
  Do the Argentines up brown,
  Catch them with their pampas down,
And let the world enjoy a little *opéra comique!*"

JUNE 30, 1982, DISTAFF NONEPITAPH

The ERA went down today,
  a gallant little craft
whose deck was made a total wreck
  by Phyllis Schlafly's shaft.

And yet, 'tis said, it is not dead—
  just waiting for the chance
to stage a purge and reemerge
  with ERAdiance.

EXXON SUNNYSIDE UP

Exxon's profits have risen by 120 percent in the last quarter
to a high of $1.15 billion. (1978 News Item)

One must surely exxonerate Exxon
For showing so splendid a rise;
It proves that one can't put a hexx on
American free enterprise.

Though the summer was rather a bummer
For the helplessly gasless civilian,
Exxon marched to a different drummer
For a profit exxceeding a billion.

This winter, come hell or high water,
It's "eating or heating," one hears—
Plus an even more lucrative quarter
For Exxon and all of its peers.

And while Carter may earnestly hustle
To curb the wild windfall by taxx,
Exxon, flexxing its corporate muscle,
Will make certain that taxx gets the axxe.

THE SHIFT-OF-POWER HOURS

After the Ford-Carter Debates

Twixt election and inauguration
    Came a time of delicious remission
From political preoccupation
    That was known as the State of Transition.

Came an end to haranguing and clangor
    And a quick wiping clean of the slates
That allowed us to look back in languor
    Recalling the TV debates:

How grave Jerry and wide-smiling Carter
    Emerged from the first without scar
But could hardly have been Poles aparter
    When the next became Ford's debate *noire*.

How at last, although Ford kept his footing,
    Laryngitis diminished his force,
Which concluded the campaign by putting
    The Carter before the hoarse.

At the end, those who took Jimmy lightly
    As a highly unpromising starter
Considered him more reconditely
    As the new and the true *Magna* Carter . . .

But his clout began losing its vigor
    When he got into jam after jam
Till he seemed a Voltairean figure:
    A Dixieland Candide Yam.

SPURNED KERNELS

President Zia of Pakistan Dismisses Carter's
$400,000,000 Aid Offer as Peanuts (News Item)

Says Pakistan's Zia,
"The very idea
Is far too absurd to discuss:
You people must *be* nuts
To offer such peanuts
As four hundred million to us."

"Though peanuts may do
For your Washington crew,
Your stinginess ought to abash you.
If you want us to spar
With the U.S.S.R.,
You'd better come up with the cashew!"

—AND STILL MAYOR

When Carey withdrew from political view,
 Mayor Koch felt an urge for expansion
And though happy at Gracie, decided (in précis)
 To move to the governor's mansion.

When he asked, "How'm I doin'?" pols said,
 "You're a shoo-in.
Cuomo's campaign is the bunk."
But suddenly Koch found he'd made a bad botch
 When he talked to a *Playboy* quidnunc.

Though a notice in *Playboy* quite possibly may buoy
 Prestige, it can ravage the vote,
Koch found to his peril when "Suburbs are sterile"
 Became his most damaging quote.

In addition, it seems, he had gone to extremes
 In deriding the voters upstate,
Which changed "How'm I doin'?" from shoo-in to ruin
 By the time of the primary date.

This left Koch without *bon mot* when "*Ecce Cuomo!*"
 Came trumpeting out of the blue
And the mayor's ambition for higher position
 Collapsed into Koch 22.

THE BYRNING OF CHICAGO:
JANUARY 1982

Though Chicago's mayor was feisty, sour, and cold
    as lemon iced-tea,
  She'd been spicing up the Second City mix.
From the moment that she leapt in, Mrs. Byrne has been
    adept in
  The farrago of Chicago politics.

When elected by a blizzard, she immediately scissored
  All connection with her mentor's old machine,
Which had long been out to get her, but she did
    the boys one better
  With a verve that left the scene incarnadine:

Having learned from Mayor Daley how to swing a mean
    shillelagh,
  She wrought havoc from the day she made her bow
Till she seemed to be aspiring to a Great Chicago Firing
  That would top the work of Ms. O'Leary's cow.

Moving past the nitty-gritty, she took action
    in the city,
  Improved its schools and moved into a slum,
Where her stay, however brief, brought on poverty
    relief,
  Leaving most of her detractors stricken dumb.

Faced with reelection scrimmage, she revamped
    her public image,
    (Her appearance had been somewhat *laissez-faire*),
Switched her style from flouncy-cute to the sharply
    tailored suit,
    After which she started Byrnishing O'Hare.

Though Chicago'd been exciting since its mayor
    came out fighting,
    Getting pelted with both brickbats and bouquets,
Would the stew that she'd been brewing
    keep constituents accruing
    Or exhaust the city's taste for *Sauce Byrnaise?*

MAL DE MAYOR

"Can it be, Mayor White," a Bostonian said,
    "That you've been in your office too long?"
"Malarky!" said White with a toss of his head,
    "In my fourth term I'm still going strong."

"You *started* off strong, sir," his critic replied,
    "In the midst of the Hub's hurly-burly,
And all our best citizens viewed you with pride—
    Till your hair grew suspiciously Curley."

"In my youth," answered White with a smile, "I concede
    That to many I seemed a Disraeli,
But I thought it more prudent to follow the lead
    Of Chicago's late great Richard Daley."

"Can it be your machine, then, that raised so much cash
    For that party you planned for your wife?"
"Ancient history!" Kevin snapped back in a flash.
    "The press wields a rusty old knife."

"More recently, Mayor," his critic began,
    But White interrupted with vigor,
"The Whitewater rapids I've shot, my good man,
    Have made me a national figure."

The critic persisted: "Of late, Mr. Mayor,
    You've been clean out of reach, out of sight.
Has your spirit gone glimmering off on a tear
    To some distant, remote Isle of White?"

Quoth the mayor, "It's clear that you don't comprehend
  Municipal tangles and snarls.
I trust that you'll promptly oblige me, my friend,
  By taking a leap in the Charles."

In D.C., de la Renta's become front and center
  With Galanos, Gucci, and Blass,
While mink and chincilla now filla the billa
  For chic in the governing class.

But the elegance trend may depend in the end
  On the cuts for which Reagan is pressing
With such passionate fire they may well inspire
  A fashion for surgical dressing.

LEAVES OF CRASS

Our Poets View Reagan's Policies: March 1981

JAMES WHITCOMB RILEY

When supply-side gits the bacon
  And demand-side's up the crick,
It can start a heap uv achin'
  In the body politic.

And when all them truly needy
  Git their safety nets an' stuff,
That'll make the merely seedy
  Truly needy quick enuf.

HENRY WADSWORTH LONGFELLOW
(*With a touch of Frost*)

"Tell me not in mournful figures
  How your costs of living rise,
Watch the way my program triggers
  Fabulous free enterprise.

"I will get you out of hock, man,
  Just believe it heart and soul:
Once you've started taking Stockman
  Things will be in decontrol.

"What if Haig is rattling sabers
  With more fervor every day?
'Good offenses make good neighbors,'
  As the poet used to say."

EDGAR ALLAN POE

Once upon a looming crisis
Brought about by zooming prices,
Expectational inflation seeping slowly through the floor,
Came the budget cuts, proceeding
Expeditiously, unheeding
Any special-interest pleading—save about El Salvador.
When implored to reconsider, reevaluate, restore,
Quoth the Reagan, "Nevermore!"

A REAGAN PRIMER

I

School days, school days,
Segregated school days,
As Goldsboro Christian and Bob Jones U.
Ran Pennsylvania Avenue,
Holding a status exempt from tax
To bolster their pious contempt of blacks
Till Reagan, amazed by undreamt attacks,
Saw he'd committed a flub.

II

Rub-a-dub-dub, three men in a tub,
Which of the trio took blame for the flub?
Not Deaver, not Baker.
'Twas Ed Meese-chief-maker
Who came out as Beelzebub.

III

Then Rockabye Ronnie, doing a flop,
Said, "It's with me the buck's gonna stop.
There's been a small procedural flaw.
I'll just have Congress fix up a law."

IV

With a will
He climbed the Hill
To fetch some legislation,
But Hatch then natch
With great dispatch
Maneuvered its frustration.

Then indeed
In dire need
To quiet the condemner,
As last resort
Ron used the Court
As dump for his dilemma.

UP A TREE

I think that I shall never see
So weird a foreign policy

As Haig, with arrogance sublime,
Was perpetrating in his prime,

Preempting out-and-out control
Of Weinberger's allotted role

While plotting nuclear "look see"
To terrify the enemy

And scheming to dispatch a corps
To straighten out El Salvador,

As day by day his policy
Haigspanded more Haiggressively. . . .

The world has not been quite the same
Since Haig played God—and lost the game.

THE WRECK OF REAGAN'S
FIRST BUDGET PLAN

It was the listing Ship of State
That cut the raging sea,
With its supply-side running low
On Social Security.

Its skipper, standing staunch, refused
To contemplate a switch
From his announced intent to aid
The truly needy rich.

"Oh, Skipper!" his advisers cried,
"A storm is on the way."
"I've weathered storms before," quoth he,
"In Cal-i-for-nye-aye.

"I have no doubt you'll tell me next
That eastern skies look cloudy
And counsel me to trim my sales
Of AWACS to the Saudi."

"But, Skipper, in the Congress now
The tide's in confluence
To raise Entitlement and cut
Vast billions from Defense."

"'Twould squeeze such gripes from Weinberger . . . !"
He said in repartee,
"Let's just deep-six Entitlement
And departments that start with *E*.

"My course is set, my mandate firm
As your intrepid Skipper,
So give your blood and sweat and tears
To win this for the Gipper!"

O who will save the Ship of State
As it sweeps along to grief,
With its Budget, like the Hesperus,
Headed straight for Stockman's reef!

ELEGY TO THE COUNTRY'S OUT-OF-STOCKMAN

The curfew sounds the knell of parting Dave. . . .
Though still he's in that "happy family group,"
Secure within the Oval Room enclave,
His credibility's begun to droop.

Whoever could have guessed it in advance?
Dave spoke with such conviction on the tube
And twiddled with the national finance
As if it were his private Rubik Cube

Ignoring cries of "Stockman, spare that cut!"
Unhampered by the need to be humane,
He went right on to engineer a glut
Of social programs swirling down the drain.

He doubtless would have soared in happy flight,
His rise unchecked and splendidly exchequered,
If he had curbed his breakfast appetite
To do a little talking off the record.

MORAL:
Young man, if you choose to be key to the news
And recorded as more than a yes-man,
You must carefully purge that insidious urge
To share all your thoughts with a pressman.

Though you're cockily sure that your fame is secure,
Yet you feel that such talk might abet it,
Since your tongue is so talented—do as Dick Allen did:
File it away and forget it.

Things were looking pretty rocky for the Reagan team
of late
With a trio of its superstars about to get the gate.

Behind the woodshed, Stockman stood for fouling up
the pitch:
Instead of making history, he made a mammoth glitch.

Behind the eight ball, Richard Allen felt it was a shame
To bench a fellow just because he played too "safe"
a game.

The third man up on waivers was the CIA's Bill Casey,
Who offered such lacunae in his business record précis

That it seemed as if his memory were something of
a sieve.
But the Senate called him safe at first—by double
negative.

And the prospects of the Reagan team have cleared up
quite a bit.
Today there's joy in Mudville: Casey ranks as
"not unfit."

CLOTHES QUESTION

June 4, 1982. Nancy Reagan appears at an Economic Summit Reception wearing black satin-banded knickers.

Whenas to Paris Nancy goes
   She does not underdress
But takes along the kind of clothes
She feels will bring out Ahs and Ohs
And possibly *Bravissimos*
   From public and from press.

So while her husband deals and dickers,
   Taking solemn stands,
Popular attention flickers
As the hordes of camera-clickers
Concentrate on Nancy's knickers
   With their satin bands.

The knickers, having had display
   In pictures fore and aft,
Did Nancy, as has been her way
Convey them to the Louvre *Musée?*
If so, perhaps, upon that day
   The Mona Lisa laughed.

REAGANALYSIS

People say I've gone back to a pre-New Deal tack
And deplore my recidivist quirks,
But, friends, it's a cinch that I won't give an inch!
I have seen the past—and it works!

VINTAGE '81

Though the year '81 was no barrel of fun,
It had moments deserving of savor:
Paradoxical nips that could pucker the lips,
With their pungent oReagano flavor.

Reagan tilted a lance at the nation's finance
And assured us the cash flow would freshen,
But it took a deep swerve from the famed Laffer curve
To a state of Stockmanic depression.

If Ron seemed too unskilled for a woodworkers guild
When he started his Cabinet-making,
Still in Congress the Yeas that he managed to raise
Were decidedly Democrat-shaking.

The programs he urged left the out-party purged,
As he brought new adherents to heel,
Till the daily upheavals of swarming Boll Weevils
Covered all but the Tip of O'Neill.

Meanwhile Haig went to bat with "I'll caveat that,"
Making syntax appear a bit hapless,
And he took so prehensile a role in Defense
That he nearly scared Weinberger Capless.

On the distaff side: chic reached its Washington peak
With a frenzy of minks and chinchillas
(Causing more of a stir than the rather drab fur
Of the infighting White House guerrillas).

The Reagan Reign · 53

And when Sandra O'Connor was raised to "Your Honor,"
The thought couldn't fail to delight us
That she wasn't perturbed or the slightest bit curbed
By a massive attack of NewRightis.

Though 'twas poor propaganda when Ling-Ling, our panda,
Gave British-bred Hsing-Hsing the mitten,
With Diana *enceinte*, what hosannahs we chant
To the potent potential of Britain.

Although some people mull on this year as too dull,
That opinion is one that needs spiking,
For with crises in Poland, air traffic control and
Our national game—it was striking.

NEW YEAR'S ADVICE TO THE AFFLUENT FOR 1982

Gather yet tax cuts while ye may
    In glorious entrancement
Before they fade and melt away
    As "revenue enhancement."

Alas, ye fail to trickle down
    The funds ye ought to free up
And never put a nickle down
    To jack the GNP up;

Ignoring all hypotheses
    On what the well-heeled class owes,
Ye do not foster industries
    But buy yourselves Picassos.

You've bollixed Reagan's fiscal song,
    So please, no histrionics
If this year's music brings out strong
    Recessional harmonics.

CAPPING THE PIPE

Returned from Santa Barbara, Ron still appears
    to harbor a
  Disgust with all you nations that defy
The Reagan ideology by selling gas technology
  To get that Soviet pipeline into high.

He's sent you Cap the W to harass you and trouble you,
    To make you take your offer and revoke it.
Though the hope of gas may glitter, as the sanction
    threats grow bitter,
    You must put it in your pipeline, friends, and smoke it.

ARMS AND THE SALESMAN

The mideastern phrase most in vogue nowadays
With the hell-bent-on-armaments grasper
Springs from one that appears in the movie *Algiers*,
"Oh, come with me to the Caspar!"

THE RED AND THE BLACK INK

Since Jacob vied with Esau
There has never been a seesaw
Like the budget planned for nineteen eighty-two:
Up go military forces,
Down go humanist resources,
In a wild unbalanced act of derring-do.

And while Caspar, pushing weapons, sees
No possible discrepancies
Twixt arms and an economy that's burst,
With the deficit in billions,
Ronnie dances tax-cutillions
As he plays the role of Robin Hood reversed.

When he's faced with the upheavals
Of the Gypsy Moths and Weevils,
He enacts the part of lovable tough cutup
As he circumvents dissent
With the simple argument
That his critics have to put up or else shut up.

So we gradually drain
What entitlements remain
That Defense may be unstinted in its spending . . .
If we're wedded to this trend,
It would seem that in the end
There'll be far less in this country worth defending.

"SHOOT, IF YOU MUST"

At his window of vulnerability
    while the antinuke legions grow twitchy,
Reagan sits with a perdurability
    of a latter-day Barbara Frietchie.

When the U.S.S.R. mentions nuclear freeze,
    Ron counters with homemade statistics
To show that the Soviets lead us with ease
    in the basketball game of ballistics.

Ex-sportscaster Reagan regales us all
    with his practical tactical aim,
"Shoot, if you must, but don't freeze the ball
    when the Reds are ahead in the game!"

THE OLD BROKEN BUDGET

How dear to Ron's heart was his '81 budget
   Whose stalwart supply-side grew cracked and unKemped
As recovery stalled despite efforts to nudge it
   By cutting down taxes to levels undreamt.

But the '82 budget has set up a stupor
   That left the Conservatives grossly upset
As the tax hike turned into a two-Party-pooper
   And Reagan emerged as the Liberals' pet.

DIALOGUE

Oh, Mr. President,
Oh, Mr. President!
Is there something that disturbs you, Tip O'Neill?
I can't help but rage and cuss
When you blame your woes on us!
Tip, that tactic makes a great campaign appeal.

Oh, Mr. President!
What now, O'Neill?
Your statistics are more fanciful than real.
I may quote a figure which
Is an unimportant glitch
But the voters don't catch on; it's no big deal.

Oh, Mr. President,
Oh, Mr. President,
Though you slither out of problems like an eel,
Unemployment's looking bleak.
But EMPLOYMENT'S at its peak!
Pettifoggery, Mr. President!
Demagoguery, O'Neill!

FRUSTRATION

Ron couldn't quite fathom the reason
Why Congress officiously blocked his propitious
And palpably Peacekeeping effort to wish us
A Merry MXmas, preseason.

FUNERAL PERORATION

People thought that Ron should pop off
For a visit to Andropov,
  Of which he was undoubtedly aware,
But he wouldn't shed a tear
Into poor old Brezhnev's bier
  So he made the rite a mere Bush-league affair.

ADIEU, '82

The year '82 having vanished from view,
   It's time for a bit of reflection
On some of its commoner facts and phenomena,
Culled with cursorial, quasi-memorial
   Highly capricious selection.

The year's end was wracking as lame ducks aquacking
   Were filling the Capitol Dome,
And the sentiments voiced made it clear they were hoist
On their own petrol—flustered, harassed, filibustered . . .
   Small wonder that E.T. go home.

'Twas a year of finance, which led Ronnie a dance
   Through the rough Reaganomical shoals,
But he flouted their rigors with fanciful figures,
Raised high his Defenses, quite lost his consensus,
   And ended up sliding down polls.

He liked shooting the breeze about nuclear freeze,
   Which he linked with the Communist nexus,
But he couldn't stand soreheads who balked at his warheads
And raised so much dust that the Congress, nonplussed,
   Tied strings to his cherished MXes.

Haig, once next in command, cannot yet understand
   How he lost his control of the reins:
When he thought he had freaked out the Oval Room clique
And was sure he had Weinberger toeing the line,
   He was suddenly Capped for his pains.

But he should have assumed he'd already been doomed
   By his role in the Falkland Isles fray,
When he only lost sleep when he tried counting sheep
And got mauled in the den of Atilla the Hen
   As he sought to play Henry the K.

For the Reverend Falwell, things went not at all well:
   His enemies failed to get clipped
And the men he supported were by and large thwarted
As voters grew brighter instead of New-Righter.
   Tsk, tsk. Can it be that he's slipped?

If this captious review of the year '82,
   A year that's already extraneous,
Leaves you feeling you've missed its significant gist
And you've much have preferred it condensed in a word,
   The *mot juste* would be: missilelaneous.

XTRAVAGANZA

Our most serious problem, says Reagan,
   Is our 10-percent-plus unemployed,
      But the one that most vexes
      Him deals with MXes
   Perpetually undeployed.

GM faces similar trouble
   With its X-cars in mass disarray . . .
      They could both beat the hex
      If they put all their X
   In one basket—and threw it away.

SILVER LINING

Since their window of vulnerability failed
    To be closed by their MX corps,
Caspar and Ron, only slightly derailed,
    Have opened the Salvador.

They're planning to bring Salvadoran troops
    To be drilled at our own Ft. Bragg,
Where our expert advisers will put them through hoops
    In the game of "I capture the flag."

The happiest proof of this venture's success
    In the North Carolinian realms
Might come if these soldiers stand up to stress
    By capturing Senator Helms.

THE RUBÁIYÁT OF OMAR KHAYYÁM

(in a new translation by Secretary of the Interior James G. Watt)

A Book of Zen, a Plenitude of Pot,
A Jug of Wine, and ill-bred Loafers plot
  To foil my Plan to shape our Wilderness
But they will not defeat James Gaius Watt!

Our unused Land will bring a Tidy Sum
From those who seek Coal, Gas, Petroleum.
  I'll take the cash and let the Waste Land go
Nor heed the rumble of Opprobrium.

Environmentalists are Left-Wing Dupes
And endlessly annoying Nincompoops.
  They tried to put the Indian Sign on me.
But I, *sans* Reservation, quelled their Troupes.

The multimillion Acres I control
Are destined for an energetic Role.
  What can these mammoth Empty Lots produce
One half so precious as more Oil and Coal?

Misguided Congressmen have tried to ban
The on- and off-shore Drilling that I plan
  (So red the Rows of Democratic Fools!)
But Reagan is a most supportive Man.

My Moving Finger writes the while I vow
That I will not accommodate or bow:
  I am the Lord of the Interior!
We've had our Fill of Wilderness. Enow!

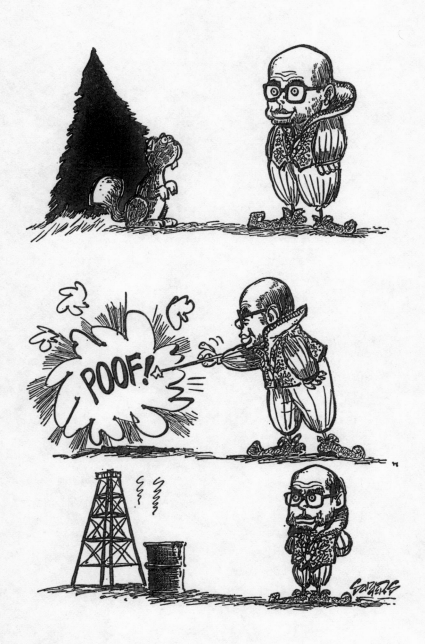